Awesome Bugs

Ants and Termites

Anna Claybourne

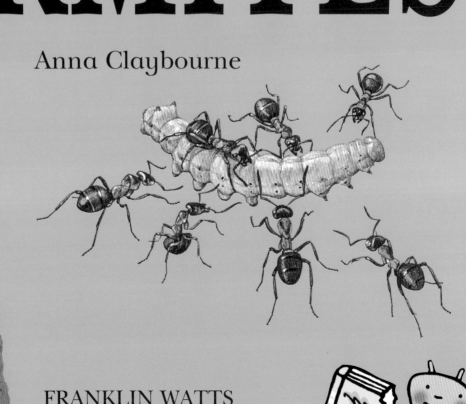

FRANKLIN WATTS
London · Sydney

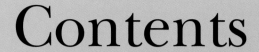

© Aladdin Books Ltd 2004

Produced by:
Aladdin Books Ltd
28 Percy Street
London W1T 2BZ

ISBN 0–7496–5793–6

First published in
Great Britain in 2004 by:
Franklin Watts
96 Leonard Street
London
EC2A 4XD

Editor:
Katie Harker

Designer: Simon Morse
Flick, Book Design & Graphics

Illustrators:
Dave Burroughs, David Cook,
Chris Shields, Tony Swift,
Myke Taylor, Ian Thompson
Cartoons: Jo Moore

Certain illustrations have
appeared in earlier books
created by Aladdin Books.

Printed in UAE

All rights reserved

A CIP catalogue record for this
book is available from the
British Library.

DUDLEY PUBLIC LIBRARIES
L   47456
659173   SCH
J595.7

Contents

INTRODUCTION 3

WHAT ARE ANTS AND TERMITES? 4

TYPES OF ANTS AND TERMITES 6

LIVING TOGETHER 9

A SHARED HOME 11

PLAYING A PART 12

BRINGING UP BABIES 15

WHAT DO ANTS EAT? 17

WHAT DO TERMITES EAT? 19

ANT AND TERMITE SENSES 21

SENDING MESSAGES 22

STAYING SAFE 25

ON THE RAMPAGE 27

WHO EATS ANTS AND TERMITES? 28

HARMFUL OR HELPFUL? 30

GLOSSARY 31

INDEX 32

Introduction

Imagine sharing your home, your food and every waking moment with hundreds, thousands or even millions of brothers and sisters! That's what life is like for ants and termites. They are incredible insects that always live together in big family groups, called colonies. By living and working together, ants and termites can build huge, complicated nests and catch food that's much bigger than themselves. Some ants and termites even grow gardens, build bridges or go to war. To find out more about these amazing animals, step inside...

Spot and count, and more fun facts!

Q: Why watch out for these boxes?

A: They answer the ant and termite questions you always wanted to ask.

zoom in on...

Bits and pieces

These boxes zoom in on ant and termite features and body parts.

Awesome facts

When you see a green diamond like this, check it out to find awesome ant and termite facts and figures.

What are ants and termites?

Ants and termites are insects – small, six-legged creepy crawlies. They belong to a special group of insects called social insects. Instead of living alone, they live together in big groups called colonies.

Awesome facts

Ants have two stomachs! One holds the ant's own food, while the other, called the crop, holds food for sharing with other ants in the colony.

Gaster, or abdomen (third and biggest body section)

2 Antennae (feelers)

Eye

Waist

Thorax (middle body section)

Legs

Mandibles (jaws)

Cleaning brush

Brain

Nervous system

Crop

Mouth

Personal stomach

INSIDE AN ANT

This picture shows a typical ant. Ants have narrow waists, and look skinnier than termites. They are usually black, red or brown. And unlike termites, most ants have good eyesight.

4

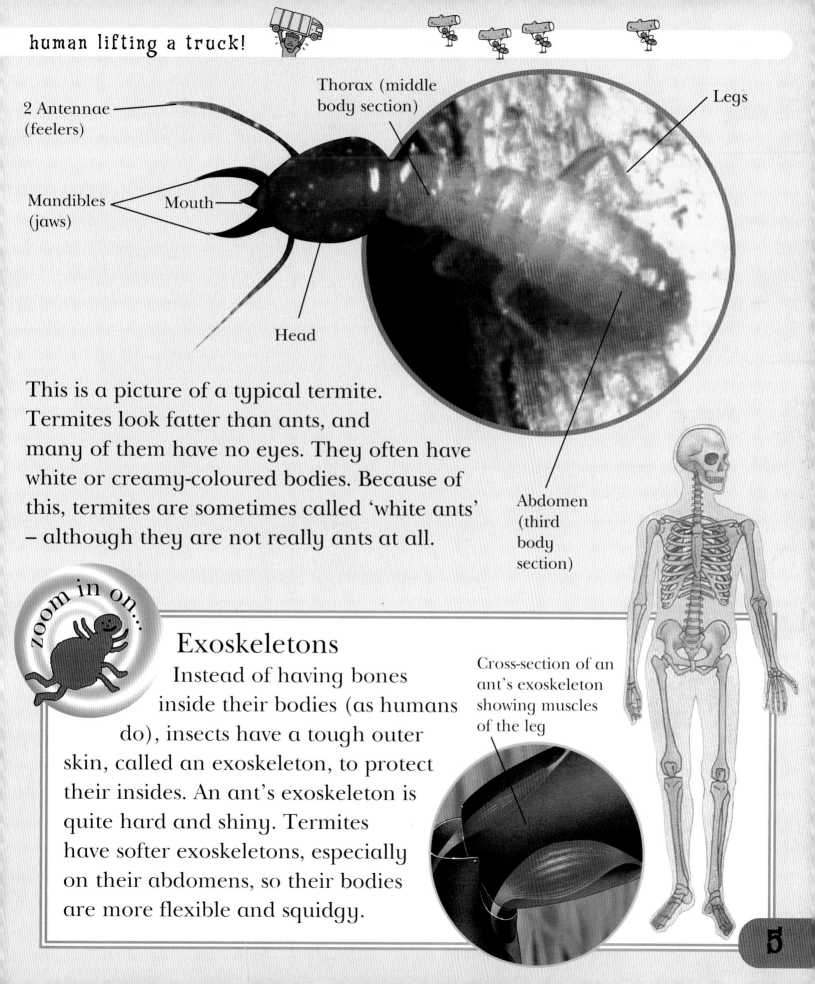

2 Antennae
(feelers)

Thorax (middle
body section)

Legs

Mandibles
(jaws)

Mouth

Head

Abdomen
(third
body
section)

This is a picture of a typical termite.
Termites look fatter than ants, and
many of them have no eyes. They often have
white or creamy-coloured bodies. Because of
this, termites are sometimes called 'white ants'
– although they are not really ants at all.

zoom in on...

Exoskeletons

Instead of having bones
inside their bodies (as humans
do), insects have a tough outer
skin, called an exoskeleton, to protect
their insides. An ant's exoskeleton is
quite hard and shiny. Termites
have softer exoskeletons, especially
on their abdomens, so their bodies
are more flexible and squidgy.

Cross-section of an
ant's exoskeleton
showing muscles
of the leg

Larva

Weaver ants are a species of ant. They build nests by fixing lots of leaves together. They glue the leaves with a kind of silk made by an ant larva (baby ant).

Weaver ants' nest

Q: Where do ants and termites live?

A: Ants live all around the world, except in a few cold or remote places such as Antarctica and Iceland. Termites like hot weather, so they live mostly in warm countries (shown in orange).

Types of ants and termites

There are more than 10,000 different species (types) of ants, and nearly 3,000 species of termites. Each species is made up of several different forms, or castes, of ants or termites – including workers, soldiers and a queen.

Young workers

Queen

TERMITE CASTES
A termite colony has three castes: workers, soldiers and 'reproductives' (which include the king and queen).

6

ANT CASTES

Ant colonies have castes, too. Like termites, they have workers and queens. Male ants die after mating, and do not become kings. And only some species of ants have soldiers.

All male ants have wings.

SPIDER ANT
Ants range from 1 mm (0.04 in) to over 3 cm (1.3 in) long, and have a variety of different body shapes. The spider ant shown above, from Australia, is very skinny, with long legs like a spider's. They help it to run fast, and it can also walk on the surface of water.

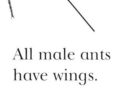

The queen is usually larger than the other ants in her colony.

Soldiers have extra-large heads and strong jaws.

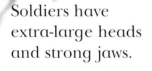

Worker

NASUTE SOLDIERS

There are two main types of termites: those that tunnel into wood, and those that burrow in the soil. Nasute termites are a type of soil-burrowing termite. Their soldiers scare off enemies by spraying them with a kind of sticky poison.

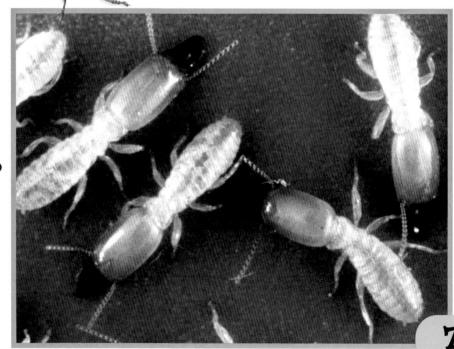

Q: Are ant and termite colonies like human cities?

A: In some ways! Colonies can have as many members as a city, but humans in a city aren't all related. And unlike social insects, humans have their own personalities.

Living together

Inside an ants' nest or a termite mound, thousands or even millions of insects live together, all sharing work and food to help each other survive. A colony is really a kind of family, because the workers and soldiers are all the queen's children.

A colony of Macrotermes termites in Africa can have more than two million members.

Army ants don't have a permanent nest, but travel together over long distances in search of food. They often march up trees to catch birds and other tree-dwelling animals to kill and eat.

ANTS TENDING EGGS

The ants in the big picture on these two pages are worker black ants inside their nest. They are busy watching over a batch of eggs the queen has laid. These will soon hatch into new ants for the colony.

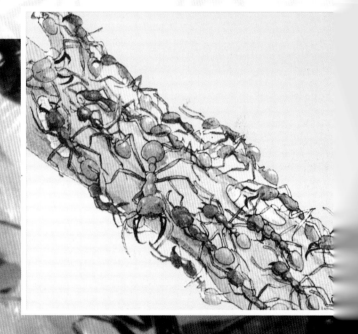

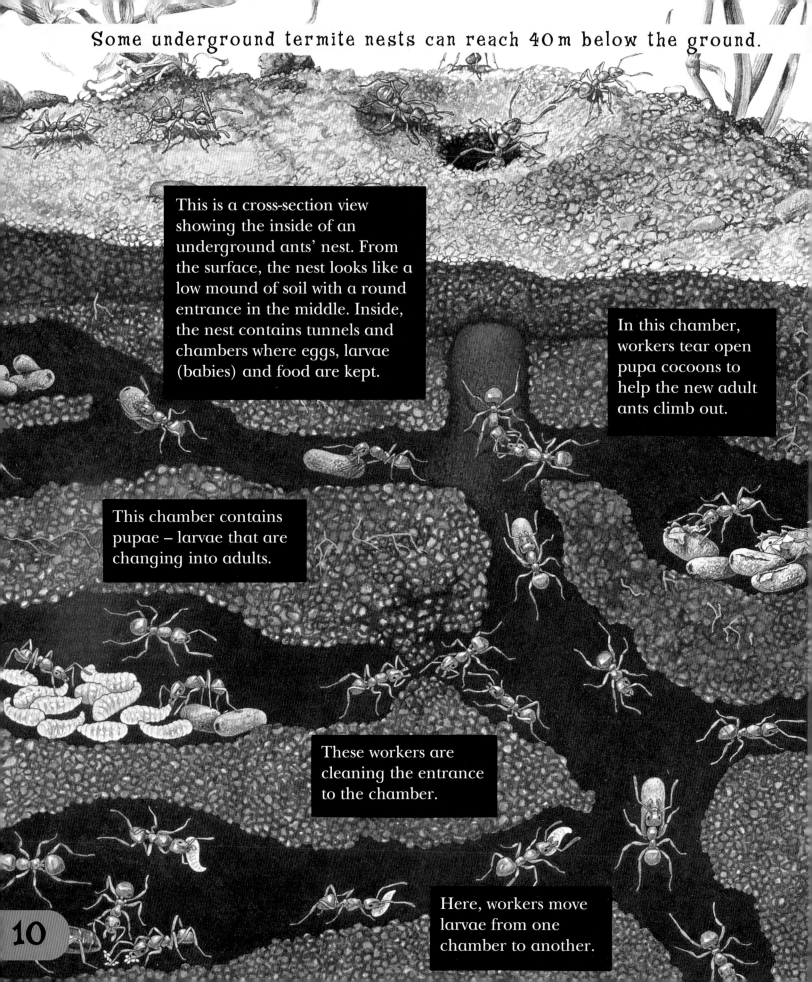

This is a cross-section view showing the inside of an underground ants' nest. From the surface, the nest looks like a low mound of soil with a round entrance in the middle. Inside, the nest contains tunnels and chambers where eggs, larvae (babies) and food are kept.

In this chamber, workers tear open pupa cocoons to help the new adult ants climb out.

This chamber contains pupae – larvae that are changing into adults.

These workers are cleaning the entrance to the chamber.

Here, workers move larvae from one chamber to another.

A shared home

Most ant and termite colonies need a home to live in. Most species make underground nests with lots of tunnels and rooms. Some termites build tall chimneys above their nests, made of soil mixed with saliva (spit) – you can see one on page 18. Some ant species make nests out of mud, leaves or even themselves!

MUDBALL ANT NEST
Some ants, such as mudball ants, build their nest in trees. They make them out of mud, soil or bits of plants stuck together, to make a round, dark-coloured ball. Mudball ants also plant seeds on their nests so that plants grow on them to camouflage them.

MUDBALL ANT

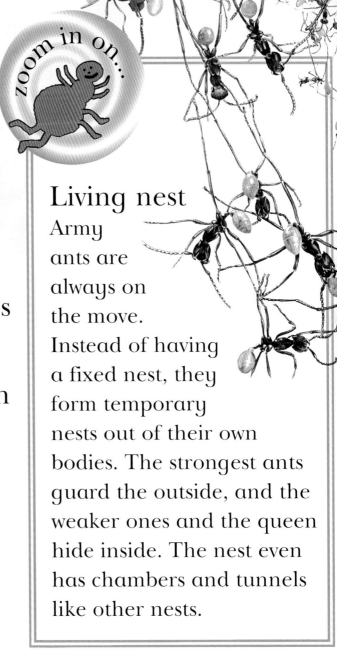

zoom in on...

Living nest
Army ants are always on the move. Instead of having a fixed nest, they form temporary nests out of their own bodies. The strongest ants guard the outside, and the weaker ones and the queen hide inside. The nest even has chambers and tunnels like other nests.

Awesome facts
Some termite towers in Africa can be more than 12 m (40 ft) high. That's like humans building a 180-storey skyscraper!

Playing a part

In an ant or termite colony, there are dozens of jobs to do, and each type of ant or termite – worker, soldier, male, king or queen – has a vital role to play. Their bodies look different because they are designed to do different tasks for the colony.

An ant queen on her nuptial flight

Male ants

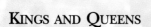

SOLDIERS
Soldier ants are bigger than workers, and they usually have very big heads and jaws for biting and fighting off enemies (such as anteaters) that attack the colony.

KINGS AND QUEENS
Ants and termites that can mate are called 'reproductives'. Queen ants begin their life with wings. A young queen sets off on a flight called a 'nuptial flight', and males fly to mate with her. After mating the queen flies to her nesting area. She loses her wings and starts a new colony. Afterwards, male ants die. Termites are different. One male mates with the queen, becomes her king and lives in the colony with her.

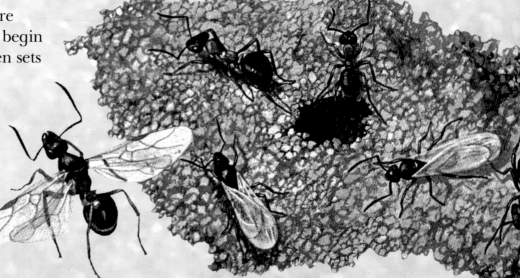

Q: How do workers know what to do?

A: It's partly instinct – a set of instructions built into each ant or termite's brain before it's born. Social insects also send each other messages using smelly chemicals. But scientists believe they don't 'think' or make decisions like humans do.

WORKERS

Workers do most of the everyday jobs in an ant or termite colony. They collect food, store it in the nest, carry new eggs away from the queen, look after the eggs, feed the babies, build new nest walls and tunnels, and keep the nest clean.

Worker ants

GIANT TERMITE QUEENS

In some termite species, after the nuptial flight, the queen grows bigger and bigger, until she is a huge, sausage-shaped egg-making machine, up to 20,000 times bigger than a worker. She is so big she can hardly move and the workers have to feed her.

Some termite queens can lay up to 30,000 eggs a day and have 100 million babies in a lifetime.

King

Workers

Queen

13

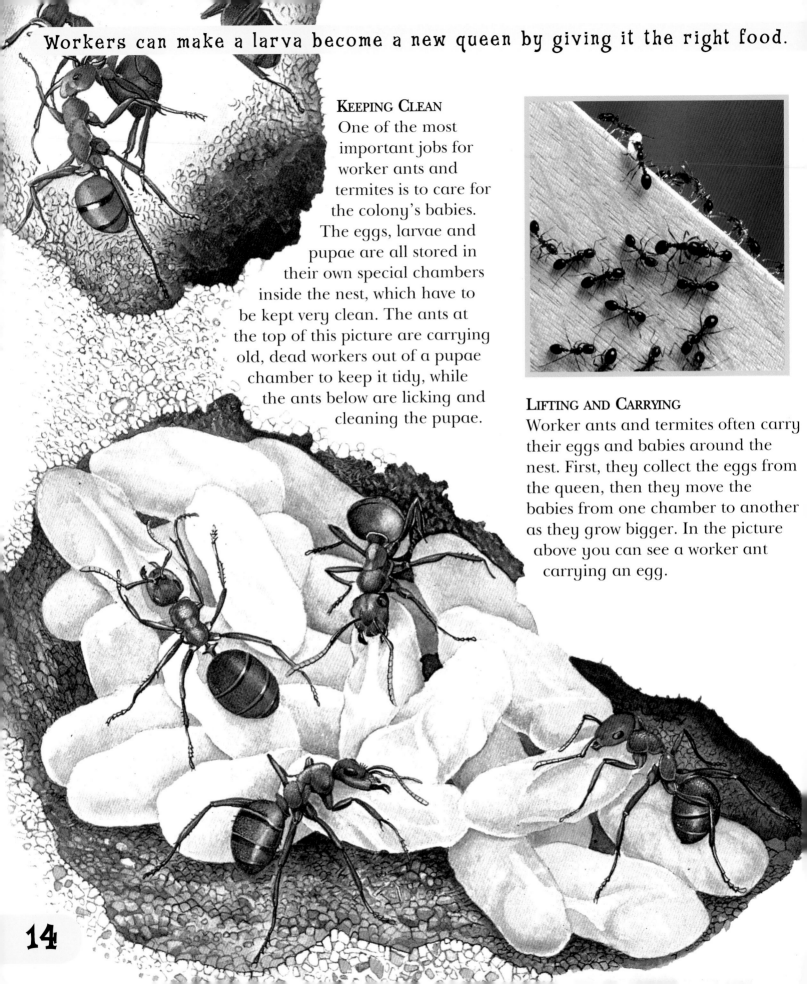

Keeping Clean

One of the most important jobs for worker ants and termites is to care for the colony's babies. The eggs, larvae and pupae are all stored in their own special chambers inside the nest, which have to be kept very clean. The ants at the top of this picture are carrying old, dead workers out of a pupae chamber to keep it tidy, while the ants below are licking and cleaning the pupae.

Lifting and Carrying

Worker ants and termites often carry their eggs and babies around the nest. First, they collect the eggs from the queen, then they move the babies from one chamber to another as they grow bigger. In the picture above you can see a worker ant carrying an egg.

Useful weaver larvae

The larvae (babies) of weaver ants do a very useful job for their colony. They make a kind of sticky thread, which the workers use to sew leaves together to make their nest. A worker holds a larva in her mouth and squeezes it to make the thread come out.

Bringing up babies

Ants and termites care for and feed their babies. But it's not the babies' mother – the queen – who looks after them. Instead it's the workers – the babies' big brothers and sisters.

WEAVER
ANTS

FOUR STAGES

Each ant or termite goes through four stages as it grows up. It starts as an **egg**, which hatches out into a **larva**. Then the larva becomes a **pupa**. The **adult** develops inside the pupa, then climbs out.

Pupa

Adult climbing out

Eggs

Larva

TAKING SLAVES

A slavemaker ant queen (the red ant in this picture) invades another ants' nest and takes over its pupae. When they hatch out, they become slaves who care for the queen.

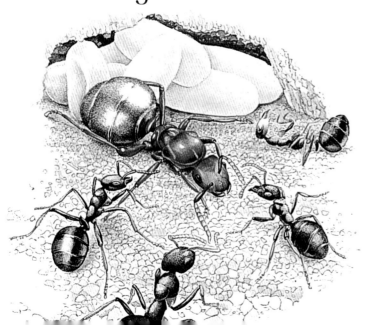

15

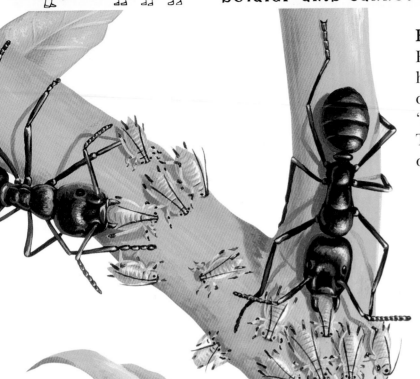

Soldier ants cannot eat because their jaws are too big.

HONEY ANTS

Honey ants collect nectar from flowers, and honeydew, a sweet liquid made by insects called aphids. Inside the nest, some of the ants, called 'honeypot' ants, act as living storage jars. Their bodies swell up to hold lots of honeydew and nectar as a food supply for the colony.

When they are storing food, honeypot ants hang from the roof of their nest.

Q: Do ants eat humans?

A: Some ants, such as fire ants, have been known to attack humans. To ants, a human is just another kind of animal – if they can kill one, they may eat it. But this is rare and only happens with a few species.

Workers have to feed them.

What do ants eat?

Most ants are omnivores – they eat all kinds of food. Many species are fierce hunters. They kill and eat other insects and even larger animals, such as deer. Some feed on dead, rotting animals, and many raid our food supplies, too.

LEAFCUTTER ANTS
Leafcutter ants have very unusual food. They collect pieces of leaves, then store them and grow a kind of fungus on them. The fungus is the ants' food.

FORAGING
To find food, ants leave their nest and go on foraging trips. They travel together in a long line, using a trail of scent to make sure they all go the same way.

Although ants are tiny, there are so many of them that they eat more meat than lions, tigers and all other big hunters put together!

Some termites eat books! Books are made of paper

Some termites use the food they collect to feed a fungus (similar to a mushroom). The fungus is grown in a 'fungus garden' inside the nest, and used as food for the colony.

1 Main chimney

2 Fungus garden

3 Queen's chamber

4 Larvae galleries

The picture shows termites feeding on rotten wood. They feed by scraping away a tiny amount of wood with their jaws. Then they carry it back to the nest inside their stomachs.

In this cross-section picture, you can see the fungus garden and other chambers inside a large termite mound.

18

which is made of wood — termites' favourite food.

What do termites eat?

Termites are vegetarians. They eat wood and rotting plant material. Some species burrow in the soil to find bits of dead wood. Others collect stalks and twigs from plants or crops, or nibble at wooden buildings, making them fall down.

Just like ants, termites leave all their food-collecting trips to the workers. As well as collecting food for themselves, the workers bring food back to the nest to feed the king, queen and young termites.

1

zoom in on...

Termite digestion

Wood is hard to digest, as it contains a tough substance called cellulose. To help them digest it, termites have tiny bacteria living inside them. The bacteria break the cellulose down into chemicals the termite's body can use.

Awesome facts

When a large termite colony attacks a wooden house, it can munch through more than a kilo of wood every day.

19

These ants have found a dead bee to use as food.

Ants hunt for food by foraging in many directions from their nest, and running around until they find a food source. When they have found one, they lay a scent trail that helps the other ants to find their way to and from the food in a straight line.

zoom in on...

Antennae

All ants and termites have two antennae (feelers). They can pick up smells and tastes from the air, and they are also used for feeling things. Ants often touch each other's antennae when they meet, as a way of telling each other where to find food – perhaps by passing on the scent of the food or the place where it was found.

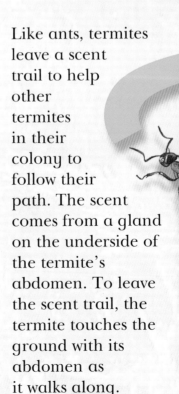

Like ants, termites leave a scent trail to help other termites in their colony to follow their path. The scent comes from a gland on the underside of the termite's abdomen. To leave the scent trail, the termite touches the ground with its abdomen as it walks along.

Scent gland

Ant and termite senses

Ants and termites need their senses to help them find food and find their way to and from their nest. Most ants can't see very well, and many termites are totally blind. Instead of eyes, their most important sense organs are their antennae, used for feeling, smelling and tasting.

Close-up of a termite's head

Close-up of an ant's head

Most ants have two eyes called compound eyes, made up of many smaller eyes joined together. However, they are not very powerful. Some termites, especially those that spend their whole lives underground, have no eyes at all.

This diagram shows a worker ant's route as it goes out searching for food, and its route on the way back to its nest. Other ants from the colony will be able to follow the route to the food by smelling the first ant's scent with their antennae.

Return journey

Outward journey

21

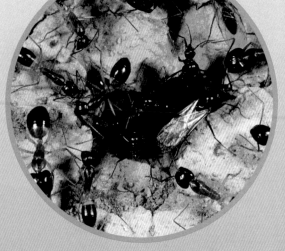

Sending messages

Social insects such as ants and termites have to work together to survive. They have to communicate, or send messages to each other, to keep the colony working. But they can't talk in words like humans can. Instead, they use sounds, movements, and special smells called pheromones.

Ants and termites are constantly touching each other with their antennae to pick up signals. The ants above are passing messages to each other as they pass in and out of the entrance to their nest.

Q: What are pheromones made of?

A: Inside their bodies, ants and termites make pheromones out of natural chemicals. Different mixtures of chemicals make different pheromones. Other animals make pheromones too, including cats, snakes and humans.

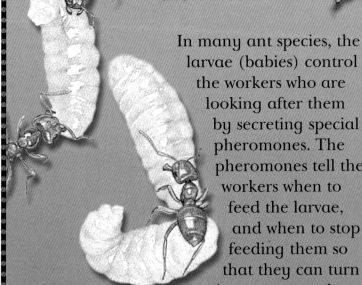

In many ant species, the larvae (babies) control the workers who are looking after them by secreting special pheromones. The pheromones tell the workers when to feed the larvae, and when to stop feeding them so that they can turn into pupae and develop into adults.

Ants caring for larvae

they want food.

In an ant or termite colony, the queen releases pheromones to send instructions to the workers. For example, one type of pheromone tells the workers that she is laying eggs for them to collect.

Ants surround their queen

Next time you find some ants, look closely to see if you can spot them touching their antennae together to 'talk'.

Members of a termite colony inside their nest

Inside their nest, termites often communicate by banging their heads against the walls of their chambers or tunnels. This makes vibrations which other termites can sense. Scientists are not yet sure exactly what these messages mean.

23

SOLDIERS

Soldiers are special ants and termites whose job is to defend their colony from attackers. They usually have very strong, extra-large jaws for biting other insects, spiders, or larger animals that try to invade their nest and feed on the colony members. Just look at the size of this soldier ant's mandibles (jaws).

zoom in on...

Formic acid

Stinging ants have a sting on the tip of their tail, just like a bee sting. When they sting, they inject a chemical called formic acid, which causes a painful, itchy feeling. Some ants can even squirt formic acid at their enemies.

24

Staying safe

Ants and termites rely on safety in numbers. If some members of the colony die, the colony makes more ants or termites to replace them. Ants and termites also use stinging and biting to fight their enemies.

Fire ants bite their victims first, then turn around and sting the area around the wound to inject painful poison.

BITING AND STINGING

Although one sting or bite from an ant or termite is usually not very serious, lots of them can be very painful. If a colony is attacked, many ants and termites work together to bite or sting their enemy and scare it away.

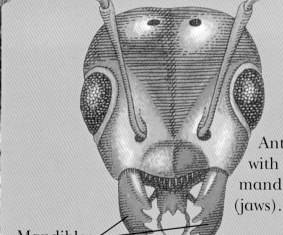

Ants bite with their mandibles (jaws).

Mandibles

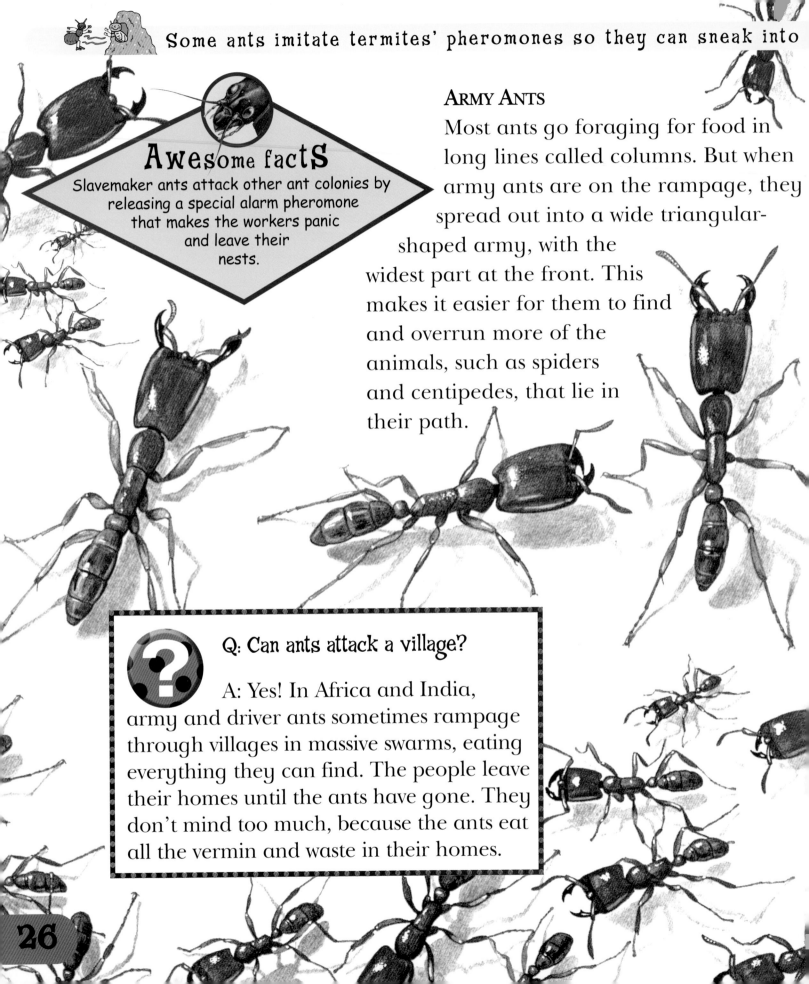

Awesome factS

Slavemaker ants attack other ant colonies by releasing a special alarm pheromone that makes the workers panic and leave their nests.

ARMY ANTS

Most ants go foraging for food in long lines called columns. But when army ants are on the rampage, they spread out into a wide triangular-shaped army, with the widest part at the front. This makes it easier for them to find and overrun more of the animals, such as spiders and centipedes, that lie in their path.

Q: Can ants attack a village?

A: Yes! In Africa and India, army and driver ants sometimes rampage through villages in massive swarms, eating everything they can find. The people leave their homes until the ants have gone. They don't mind too much, because the ants eat all the vermin and waste in their homes.

On the rampage

Because they live in colonies, termites, and especially ants, can hunt, attack and fight in groups. In fact, ants are one of the few species on Earth that form armies and go to war together.

HUNTING IN GROUPS
By attacking in a large group, these ants have managed to overrun and kill a lizard that is many times bigger than each individual ant. Some species of ants can kill even bigger animals, such as pigs and deer.

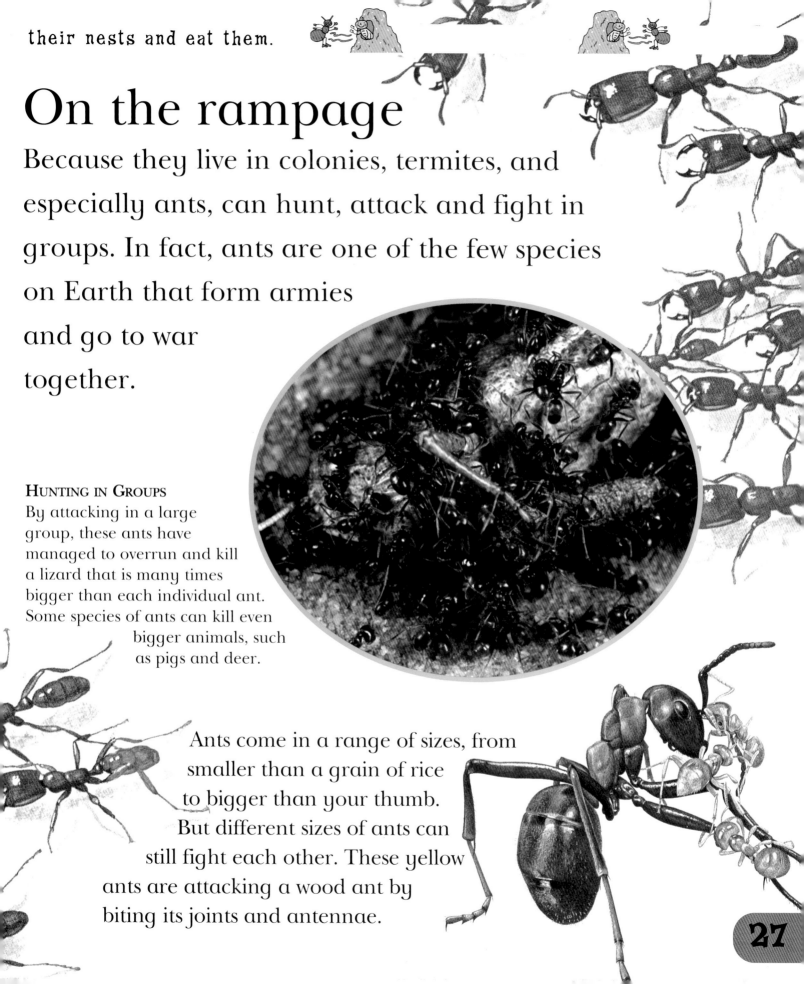

Ants come in a range of sizes, from smaller than a grain of rice to bigger than your thumb. But different sizes of ants can still fight each other. These yellow ants are attacking a wood ant by biting its joints and antennae.

27

Who eats ants and termites?

You might not like the idea of eating ants and termites, but in fact they are full of protein and make a very good food. Many animals are specially designed to feed on them – and humans can eat them, too.

The tree pangolin lives in African rainforests, and feeds on both ants and termites. It makes holes in their nests and catches them with its long, sticky tongue. It can't chew, so it swallows stones to help grind up the ants and termites in its stomach.

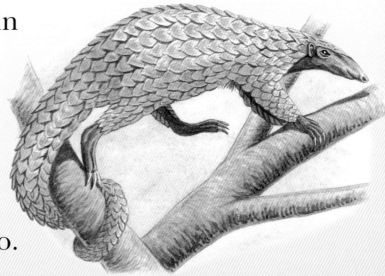

Echidnas, also called spiny anteaters (below), live in Australia. They feed at night, and like pangolins, they catch ants and termites by breaking into their nests and scooping them up with their tongues. Echidnas can sense the tiny electrical signals given off by living things. This is how they find ant and termite nests in the dark.

Anteaters get their name because they eat mainly ants, although they eat termites and other insects, too. An anteater makes a hole in an ants' nest and flicks its long tongue in and out up to 150 times per minute to catch the ants.

zoom in on...

Antlion pits

The antlion is the larva (young) of a type of insect. Antlions dig funnel-shaped pits in sandy soil, and wait at the bottom. When an ant falls in, it tumbles to the bottom of the pit, and the antlion quickly grabs it and eats it up.

Look out for chocolate-covered ants and other insect snacks in delicatessens, or when you're on holiday!

Chimpanzees in Africa like eating termites. They catch them by poking a stick into a termites' nest. Some termites climb onto the stick, and the chimp then pulls it out and licks the termites off. Scientists believe this shows that chimps are very clever. Few other animals use tools in this way.

29

Harmful or helpful?

Ants and termites can cause us problems. Ants bite and sting people and steal food, while termites burrow through wooden buildings, making them fall down. But these insects can be helpful, too. Ants help farmers by eating pests such as caterpillars, and termites break down rotting plants and recycle them into the soil.

This pictures shows the inside of a tree that has been eaten away by termites. This can be dangerous if a tree becomes so weak that it falls down.

zoom in on...

This scientist is looking at part of a house that has been destroyed by Formosan termites. These wood-nibbling termites cause huge amounts of damage every year to buildings, trees and wooden poles, especially in the southern USA. People use chemicals and metal or concrete barriers to try to stop the termites, but they are very hard to get rid of.

Fire ants

Fire ants are a pest in many countries, including Australia and the USA. They kill wildlife, chew through electric wires and have a harmful sting. Scientists are now experimenting with a type of fly that attacks fire ants, making their heads fall off (see photo right) in an attempt to control them.

Glossary

Antennae

A pair of long feelers found on the head of insects. Antennae are sense organs used for feeling, smelling and tasting.

Cellulose

The material that forms the walls of plant cells.

Cocoon

A case of spun threads that an insect larva spins around itself. The insect turns into an adult insect inside the case.

Colony

A group of animals or plants of the same kind that live together in the same area.

Crop

A second stomach found in insects and other animals without backbones. The crop is used to store food for sharing with others, or digesting another time.

Exoskeleton

The hard outer covering of some animals which gives the body its shape, and protects the organs inside.

Foraging

To go in search of food.

Gaster

The abdomen – it contains the large internal organs.

Instinct

A form of behaviour that some animals are born with.

Larva

Part of the life cycle of insects and other animals without backbones. The larva hatches out of the egg and has a soft, wormlike body.

Mandibles

The scientific name for jaws. This special mouth part is used by insects to cut and crush solid food before it is eaten.

Pheromone

A chemical with a strong smell that is sent out by an animal. It affects the way other animals behave.

Pupa

Part of the life cycle of insects and other animals without backbones. A pupa does not eat or move. It consists of a hardened case inside which the insect develops into the adult form, before it emerges.

Reproductives

Ants and termites that can mate.

Species

Living things that are very similar to each other and can breed together.

Thorax

The part of the body between the head and the abdomen. The thorax has three segments that bear three pairs of legs and one or two pairs of wings.

Index

Photocredits

Abbreviations: l-left, r-right, b-bottom, t-top, c-centre, m-middle
All pictures supplied by Otto Rogge Photography except for:
5tr, 14tr, 18bm, 20br, 30bl – Scott Bauer; ARS. 7br, 13br, 21tr, 30tr – USDA. 8br, 30tl – Photodisc. 18tm – Corbis. 23bl – Corel. 30br – Sanford Porter; ARS.